The New York Mafia:

The Origins
Of the New York Mob

The origins of the New York Mafia start with Giuseppe Masseria, AKA Joe the Boss. (Below)

Masseria was the most powerful Mafia don in New York City from 1920 till 1930, with absolute control over the Lower East Side. An old world Mafia enforcer, he fled to the US from Sicily in 1903 to avoid a murder charge that even the Sicilian Mafia couldn't fix.

Forced into hiding in New York, Masseria began work as an enforcer for the Morello organization, a Mafia gang, families had not yet been established in the United States, that operated on the Lower East Side, under the sponsorship of two ambitious gangsters, Iganzio Saietta and Ciro Terranova.

Iganzio Saietta

Ciro Terranova.

But Masseria was equally ambitious, and after Saietta was sent to prison and Terranova retired from crime, having struck it rich by cornering the national artichoke market, Masseria, within seven years, controlled an enormous part of the rackets in New York.

Masseria was an old world Mafia Don, a tyrannically, strict bigot, who ordered his top men, young gangsters like Charles "Lucky" Luciano, to stop associating with Jewish mobsters. It was, he said, "unwise" to have relationships outside the Sicilian organization.

As for the Irish gangs that surrounded him and constantly encroached into his rackets, Masseria said it was easier to kill them than to bring them into his organization. As a result, his organization was insular and almost constantly involved in a street war.

Charlie Lucky, Charles Luciano

Joe Masseria ruled supreme until 1927 when Maranzano, a native of Castellamarese del Gulfo, Sicily, came to the U.S. with permission of the Mafia Chieftain there, Cascio Ferro, with orders to bring New York under the control of the European Mafia and prepare the way for Ferro to take over.

Cascio Ferro

However Ferro was arrested by the Mussolini's fascists and imprisoned for life and never made it to the U.S, leaving Maranzano free reign in the United States.

Unlike most of the Mafia leaders of his time, who were crude and simple peasants, Maranzano, was a well-educated and somewhat refined former seminarian. He was also a brutal murderer who shot and stabbed his way into Masseria's rackets, causing the Castellamarese war, named after the town of Castellammare del Gulfo that spawned Maranzano and his young Americanized followers, Joe Bonanno; Jose Profaci; and Stefano Magaddino

Profaci

Magaddino

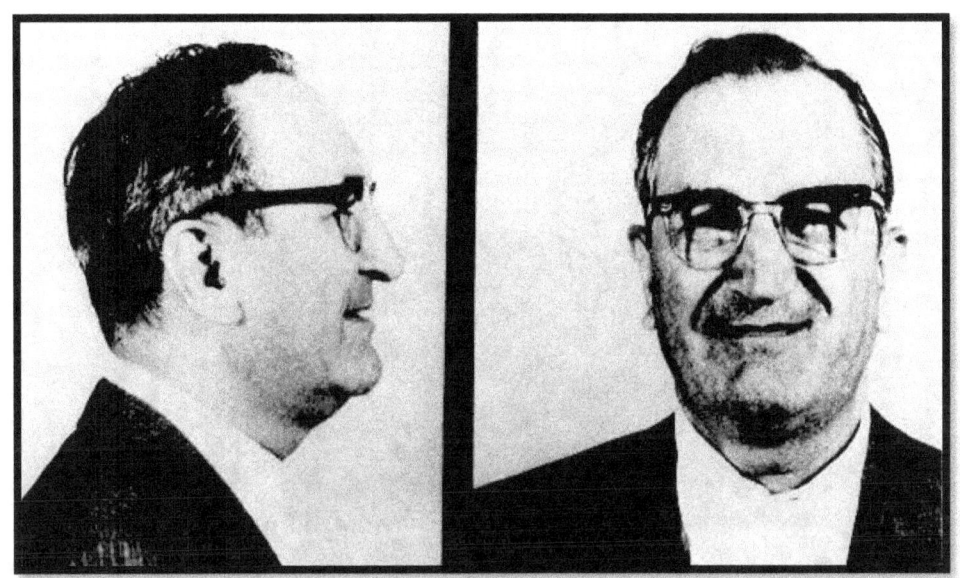

Joe Bonanno

Profaci

"LA CALA." PALERMO. (THE OLD HARBOR)

At first, an arrogant Masseria wasn't concerned with the younger Maranzano. He responded in the old way of doing things, he filled the streets with gunmen and ordered them to kill anyone associated with the Castellamarese. While that plan may have worked in Sicily, in the new world, it failed completely largely because Masseria's men were independent business people with ongoing financial interests in prostitution; narcotics, extortion and bootleg beer and street wars were extremely expensive and took them away from the more important matters.

Victims of the Castellamarese War

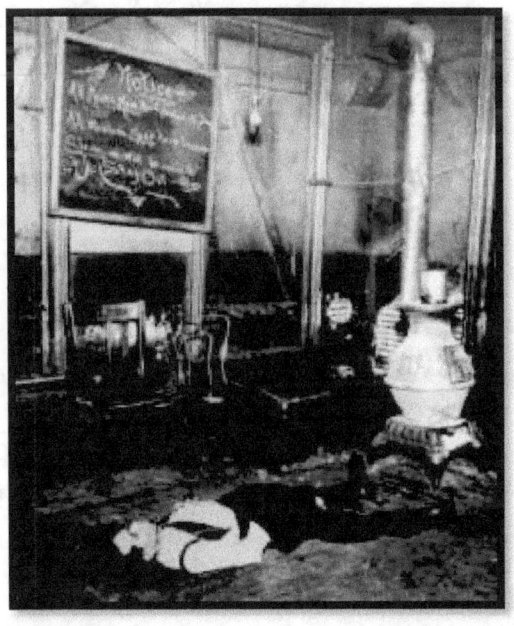

Masseria responded by bringing in new men from Italy and paying his American crews more money as a means to keep their loyalty, but eventually his war chest started to deplete. Added to that was the fact that Masseria was extremely unpopular with his crews who were reluctant to rush into an ongoing war for a man they detested largely because he refused to share his fortunes.

At the same time, the young Turks recognized the newly arrived Maranzano as just another tyrant. The leader of the Young Turks, Charles "Lucky" Luciano, decided to kill both Masseria and Maranzano and carry through with his American vision to organize crime by ridding it of the old world mentality of the so-called "Mustache Pete's" who spent their days plotting and counter plotting old world vendettas.

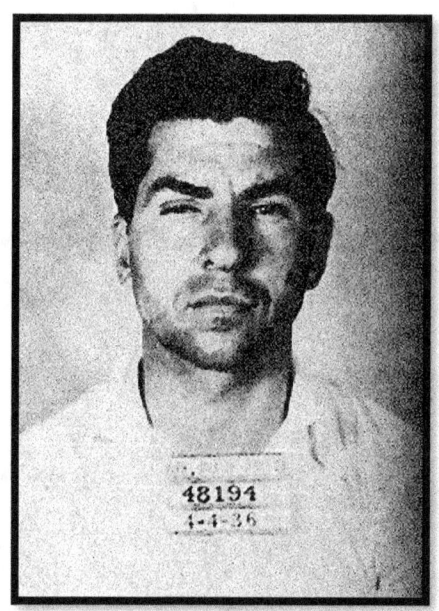

Luciano

Luciano had been working for Masseria but soon Maranzano learned of Luciano's talents and intelligence and was pleased when Luciano expressed an interest in switching over to his side. However, Luciano was as calculating and cunning as any old world Don and convinced Maranzano that he could turn over to his side while secretly remaining Masseria's employ as a sleeper agent.

Masseria

On April 15, 1931, Luciano, with Maranzano's approval, made his move. He invited Masseria to a Coney Island restaurant, The Nuova Villa Tammaro, because Masseria knew the owner and would be comfortable there. After a meal, when the restaurant was empty of customers, Luciano excused himself and went to the bathroom.

The Nuova Villa Tammaro

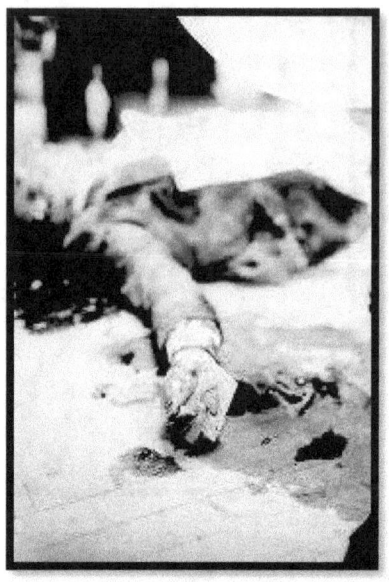

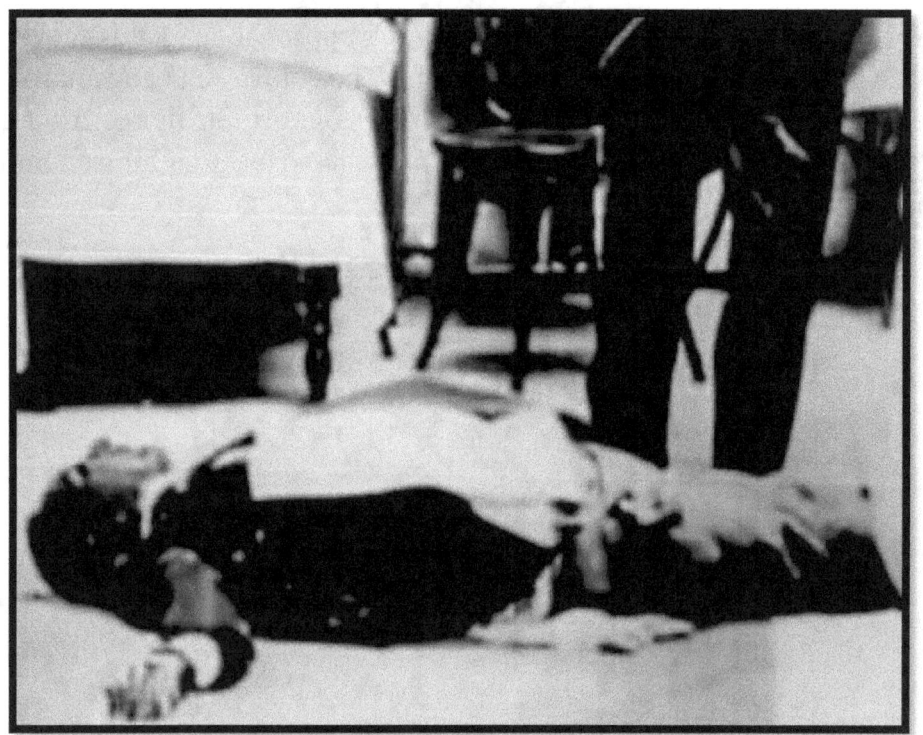

Masseria dead

Vito Genovese

As he did this, four gunmen, Vito Genovese, Joe Adonis, Albert Anastasia, future boss of what would be the Gambino crime family and Bugsy Siegel, future builder of Las Vegas, entered the restaurant shot Masseria dead. With Masseria gone, the Castellamarese War ended with a cost of between fifty to one hundred lives.

Bugsy Siegel. This was the gangsters official photo which was available for free to his guests at the Flamingo Hotel casino in Las Vegas

Maranzano now declared himself Capo di tutti Capi -- or Boss of all Bosses and called for a meeting with all the Mafia members in the United States. A huge banquet hall was rented which Maranzano had decorated with religious symbols to give off an air of reverence.

He addressed the meeting by explaining that his new organization would have five lieutenants below him and under them, crew chiefs, or Capo's and soldiers assigned to each "Crew" which would be made up of between 15 and 25 members of the Mafia, or "Soldiers". He further ruled that there would be no more vendetta killings and only those of Sicilian decent would be permitted to be involved in this organization.

Several days after the meeting, Maranzano began plotting the murder or his subordinates, especially Luciano. Others to be killed included Vito Genovese, future leader of the mob family that would bear his name, Al Capone of Chicago and Joe Adonis. To carry out the ghastly chore, Maranzano hired an independent Irish hoodlum named Vincent "Mad Dog" Coll.

Joe Adonis

Maranzano dead

The Mad Mick, Vincent Coll

At the same time, Luciano plotted his move against Maranzano. On September 10, 1931, six months after Masseria was killed and the same day that Maranzano had planned to have Luciano murdered, Maranzano was executed as he sat in his office. True to the new world order, Luciano sent Jewish thugs to carry out the murder. With Maranzano dead, Lucky Luciano was Boss and organized crime in America changed forever.

Dewy

Luciano ruled supreme for six years and as a result of his steady handed and far-sighted management, organized crime in America thrived. However, Luciano, vain and prone to the limelight, made himself a visible target to law enforcement, almost defying the authorities to curtail his power.

On January 31, 1936, a bitter cold day, New York's city police, acting on orders of District Attorney Thomas E. Dewey, went out in force and rounded hundreds of prostitutes and brought them in for questioning concerning their business relationships with the mob. In effect, what Dewey was trying to do was to build a RICO case against Luciano.

NDAY, JUNE 8, 1936

It was said that the Mar-rganized a rifle club as a so that Black Legion mem-might practice target shoot-

ge Chenot insisted that the nan grand jury will be con-ed under strict conditions of cy, and said that any witnesses discuss their testimony after have left his court room will held in contempt of court and ated accordingly." lso, any one who talks to a y witness who is under subpena appear will be held in contempt "There will be no ballyhoo in nnection with this grand jury in-... Judge Chenot said. ...tion," ...ducted strictly along ...the Michigan

Jury Convicts N. Y. Vice Ring

Finds Nine Leaders of Gang Guilty

NEW YORK, June 7—(U. P.)—
A "blue ribbon" jury early today
convicted millionaire Charles
(Lucky) Luciano and eight co-lead-
ers of the country's biggest vice
ring on 62 counts of compulsory
prostitution.
Sentences, to be pronounced by
Supreme Court Justice Philip J.
...k at 10 a. m. June 18, may
...24 years to 1,240 years

G.O.P. Pri
Shun Co

Borah Due, by
Knox Are N

CLEVELAND
Only one of
avowed candid
lican presiden
pected to atte
vention.
Senator Bo
morrow mo
Landon pla
in Topeka,
Frank Kn
would be
for them
by teleph
Most o
horses o
preside
...thor- Senato

Dewey found his witnesses in five prostitutes, with the dubious street names of Jennie the Factory, Sadie the Chink, Frisco Jean, Nigger Ruth and Gashouse Lil. The women were held in the House of Detention as material witnesses on $10,000 bond each. Under severe questioning, each was persuaded to mention the name Lucky Luciano in their testimony and soon a case was built against Luciano for "organizing a city wide prostitution ring." Although the mob did have financial interests in prostitution "It was," said Luciano's Underboss Frank Costello, "as organized as a flea circus."

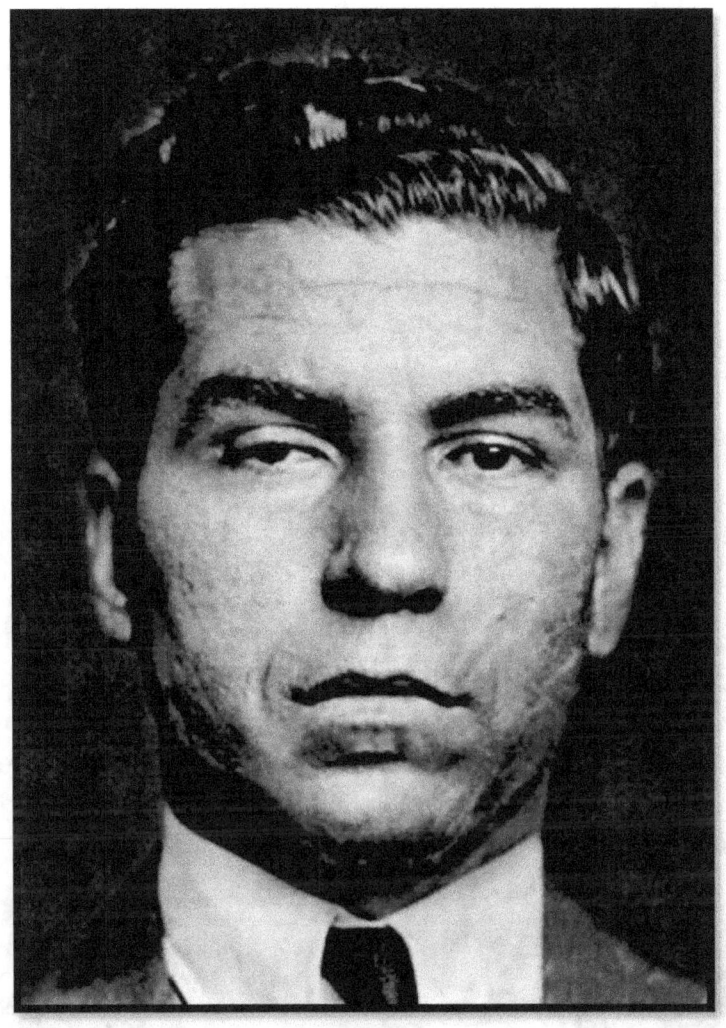

Lucky Luciano

Luciano's trial began May 11, 1936 and three pimps and several madams, one known as "Cokey Flo" turned state's evidence against the crime boss, although it now appears that most of the evidence was fabricated.

Florence
"Cokey Flo"
Brown

Dewey told the jury, "Frankly, my witnesses are prostitutes, madams, heels, pimps and ex-convicts...I wish to call to your attention that these are the only witnesses we could possibly have brought here. We can't get Bishops to testify in a case involving prostitution. And this combination was not run under the arch lights of Madison Square Garden. We have to use the testimony of bad men to convict other bad men."

During the trial Dewey asked Luciano if he had obtained his permit to carry a pistol under false pretenses. Luciano replied he had not. That he needed the gun to go hunting with.
"And what is it that you hunt in New York City, Mr. Luciano?"
"Peasants," replied the bored Luciano.

With a mountain of questionable evidence against him, the jury found Luciano guilty and sentenced him to a 35-year sentence. The conviction shocked the underworld. Twenty years later mob informant Joe Valachi said "I was stunned. Charlie Lucky, he wasn't no pimp, he was a boss."

Luciano languished in a New York State prison for almost seven years, freed, oddly enough by the events of the Second World War. By 1942, German U-boats had sunk over almost 70 vessels, mainly freighters carrying valuable and essential cargo en route to and from New York to the war effort in Europe. The attacks were exact and final, and it appeared that the Nazis knew every attacked ship's schedule and freight. US Naval Intelligence suspected that German and Italian spies were operating along the New York docks and were forwarding the shipping routes to the Axis powers. Intelligence Officers, working on vague and still unexplained orders from the War Department (The orders are still sealed and classified Top Secret) approached Manhattan District Attorney Frank Hogan and ordered his office to place them in contact with Mob Boss Vito Genovese, who controlled the docks so they could use Genovese's men as a Counter Intelligence network.

Charles Haffenden the Naval Reserve Office who ran B-3 investigating section of the district intelligence office and cut a series of dea with the mob

Talks between the Mob leaders and the Navy went on for several months. Sensing the importance of the matter, and as a means to secure a position with the Military, the Mafia actually created their own sabotage by sinking, in February of 1942, the French luxury liner Normandie, at its berth on a west side pier.

The sinking liner Normandie

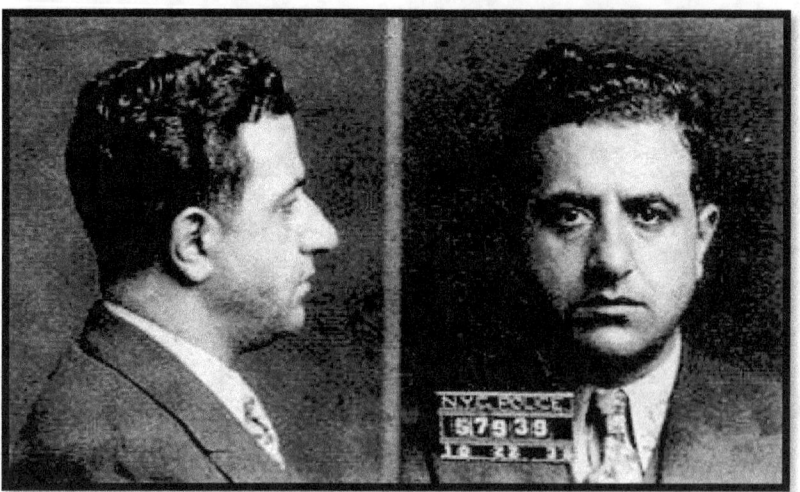

The Mad Hatter, Albert Anastasia

Albert Anastasia apparently carried out the work on Lucky Luciano's orders.

The sinking made international headlines and the Navy placed all its efforts into securing the dock and a deal was finally reached between Naval Intelligence and Joseph "Socks" Lanza, a semi-literate hood who controlled the Fulton Fish Market, then the biggest fish wholesale outlet in North America.

Lanza, right front

Lanza agreed to cooperate and offered to help Naval Intelligence agents infiltrate the market and set up listening and communications devices in fishing boats, however, he said, he could only offer to help, he couldn't actually do it.

Socks Lanza

In order to put the plan to work, Lanza said he would need a direct order from the Boss, Lucky Luciano and that order would only come with a price. The price was freedom for Lucky Luciano, who was moved from Dannemora, at the extreme northwest east corner of New York State, to Sing Sing Prison, about an hour and a half outside of Manhattan.

Dannemora Prison

Sing Sing prison

Lanza

There, at a meeting attended by Underboss Frank Costello, Hoodlum mastermind Meyer Lansky, Naval Intelligence and a representative of the District Attorney's office, a deal was struck. It was agreed that, in return for his help, Luciano would get his parole at the war's end, under the condition that he accepted deportation, voluntarily, back to Italy, his place of birth.

At the wars end, the government stuck to its end of the bargain and Luciano was released from prison as agreed. And, as agreed, Luciano accepted deportation to Naples, his place of birth, although he lived there, as an infant, for less than two years in childhood.

As predicted by the mob, Luciano stayed in Naples only long enough to solidify his control over the black market there and then turned his attentions to the international scene and regaining control of his New York operations. In the early fall 1946, he received a message from the mob financial planner, Meyer Lansky that read: "December--Hotel National."

The Hotel National

"The messenger also brought me some disturbing news" Luciano later said "He said that Vito (Genovese) was start'n to act like I wasn't never coming back. He was outa jail and walk'n around my territory in New York like he owned it. And then, right on top of that, I heard from (Frank) Costello that the 'California matter' was bad. I knew right away what he meant, that Bugsy was probably tappin' the till for even more dough than I knew about..."

In October of 1946, Luciano boarded a freighter set for South America and at its first port of call (Caracas, Venezuela), he disembarked and took a private plane to Mexico City and then flew to Havana where he would attend the first full-scale meeting of the national syndicate since the Capone sponsored conclave in Chicago in 1932.

William B. Herlands, a Dewy staff lawyer investigated the Navy's deal with Luciano but got nowhere due to the Military's interference

At a general meeting, the first issue discussed was Luciano's problems with his financial advisor, Meyer Lansky. Johnny Roselli, a Chicago hoodlum once told gangster Jimmy Fratianno: "He's (Lansky) is lucky to be alive. You know he really fucked Lucky when he was deported. Meyer sent him peanuts. The only reason he's alive today is because he's under the thumb of Jimmy Blue Eyes (James Alo, Lansky's protector). Meyer makes no moves without clearing it with Jimmy Blue Eyes."

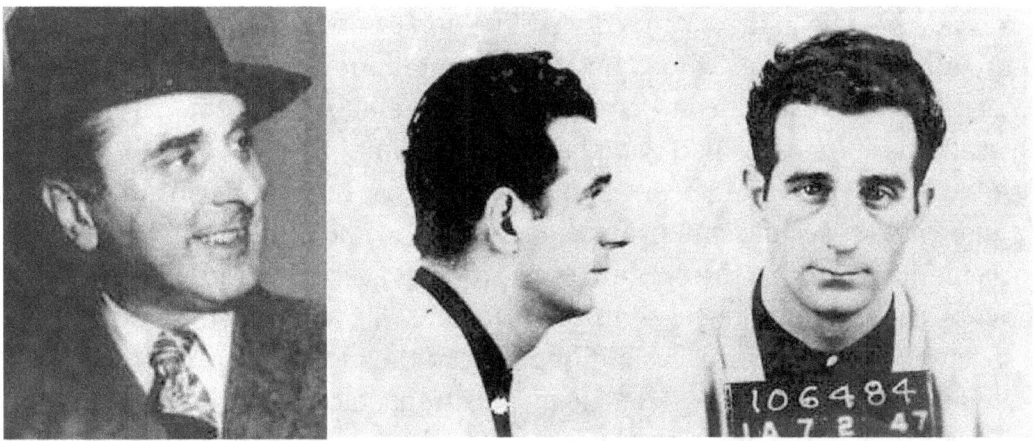

Johnny Roselli and Jimmy Fratianno

When Luciano accepted deportation to Italy, Lansky agreed and then reneged on his promises in the amounts payments he had vowed to send Luciano while he was in exile. As a result, Luciano had decided that Lansky should be killed and put out an order for his murder, but nothing happened.

Luciano in Italy

A decade in exile had greatly reduced Luciano's power base within the mob and the other mob bosses vetoed any against retaliation against Lansky, because he was, the bosses explained to Luciano, far too valuable to them.

Overall, the conference had gone badly for Luciano. Vito Genovese, soon to be Boss of a family that would bear his name, called for Luciano's retirement from the syndicate. It was his contention that Luciano would only bring on law enforcement scrutiny to the organization growing narcotics trade. He was, Genovese said, better off retired in Italy. No vote was taken on the issue, but the message was clear. Luciano was out of power in the mob.

Luciano, however, refused to cede his position, stating that he fully intended to remain active in the organization by making his base in Cuba where he would direct the organization importation of narcotics into the states from Asia and Europe. Genovese didn't like it. When he returned to the States, the Mob boss

phoned his contacts in the press and told them that that Lucky Luciano was operating in Cuba, only 90 miles off the American coastline, and that he intended to use the island as his base of vengeance to flood the United States with addictive narcotics. Within a month, the State Department put enough pressure on Cuba's President Batista to have deported back to Italy.

STERY BLAST
RECKS UTICA
MACHINE PLANT

'Lucky' Luciano
Is Arrested By
Police in Cuba

For all given purposes, the Havana convention did nothing more than signal the end of Lucky Luciano who lived out the rest of his days, powerless, in exile in Italy.

The mobs own President, Batista of Cuba

By 1940, Luciano's Underboss, Frank Costello, had taken over control Luciano's enormous crime family, which included five hundred soldiers and thirty caporegimes. Costello was actually the third Boss in line to take control of the family. Luciano's Underboss, Vito Genovese, fearing arrest in connection with the murder of a gangster named Ferdinand Boccia, received Luciano's approval to flee to Italy. As a result, everyone in the organization moved up a notch, including Costello.

When he took over the organization in the late 1930s, Costello called his Capo's, or captains, to his opulent suite at the Plaza Hotel and sent them in every direction across New York to conquer the city in his name. Costello gave Joe

Adonis and Willie Moretti New Jersey; Anthony Carfano got the Bronx; and Michelle Miranada was given the entire East Side.

Joe Adonis

He gave the principality of Greenwich Village to his favorite Capo, Tony Bender. To "Trigger Mike" Coppola, he doled out Harlem, the old Dutch Schultz kingdom.

Trigger Mike Coppola and Tony Bender

As a result of Costello's imperial expansionism, money poured in, tens of millions of dollars that allowed Costello to hire on more soldiers, and with more muscle than any other family in the country, he was able to control the unions that controlled the massive and lucrative piers and docks of New York and New Jersey, in effect making Costello the governor over the movement of virtually all freight in and out of the Americas.

A very young Frank Costello

By the early 1940's, his family controlled the garment industry, the construction business, trash collection, catering industry and restaurants, bars, nightclubs and theaters.

The original Godfather, Frank Costello

They placed a tax on almost everything that was made, sold, or traded anywhere in Manhattan, the Bronx, Harlem and New Jersey. They made tens of millions more from numbers, extortion, loan sharking, hijacking and the control of prostitution and the movement of narcotics. During all this time, and unlike the reigns of Luciano or Capone, during Costello's rule, there was relative peace, a feat that earned him the title of the "The Prime Minister of the underworld."

On June 11, 1946, Vito Genovese, officially the under boss to Frank Costello, came back to America, handcuffed to a federal agent. From that humble start, the history of organized crime in America would be changed forever.

Don Vito, Vito Genovese

Vito Genovese came to America from Naples in 1912, at the age of sixteen, with his family. They settled in Queens, both parents worked hard and prospered into the middle class. But Genovese had no intentions of leading the straight life. His first arrest came in 1917, for carrying a gun. During the years of Prohibition, he was arrested twice, but was released each time for lack of evidence when the witnesses failed to appear in court. By 1926, Genovese was a full- fledged gangster and partner with Luciano in a number of enterprises. They grew close, mostly because Genovese was one of Luciano's most feared enforcers. However, while Luciano had a certain charisma even a charm, Genovese was outwardly cunning, sly and devious. He was also stone cold. Joseph Valachi, the mob's informant, said: "If you went to him and told him about some guy doing wrong he would have the guy killed, and then he would have you killed for telling on the guy."

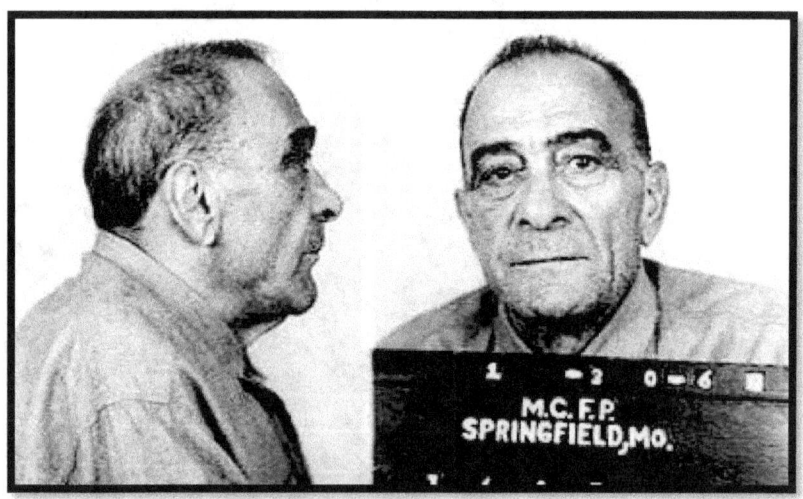

Genovese

During the early 1930s, Genovese took over New York's massive Italian lottery, and grew rich from it, using his wealth to buy into gay bars in the Greenwich Village area, which struck police as an odd choice of investments until 1954 when they learned from a cashier at one of the clubs that Genovese's wife, Anna Petillo Vernotico, who was also his distant cousin, was a regular at these clubs and for many years, was involved in a lesbian relationship which Genovese knew of, and approved.

It had always been an oddball union anyway. Genovese had married Anna a year after the death of his first wife in 1931. When he met her, Anna was locked in a loveless marriage and couldn't get a divorce. On March 16, 1932, Genovese had her husband murdered and twelve days later they were married.

Then, in 1937, Vito Genovese, under suspicion of murder of a mob soldier named Ferdinand "The Shadow" Boccia, fled the US, taking a steamer trunk containing $750,000 in cash.

Boccia dead

The Boccia murder was a study in Genovese true nature. Boccia had introduced Genovese to a rich Italian merchant whom Genovese and others conned out of a small fortune in a rigged card game. Then they sold him a machine that they said would print money.

In all, they had swindled the man of some $150,000. Boccia demanded $35,000 as his share for introducing Genovese to the merchant, and rather than pay, Genovese, already a millionaire, decided to have Boccia killed.

Prosecutor Thomas E. Dewey got the case and was closing in on Genovese when he fled to Naples and opened a narcotics export business. Genovese lived and prospered there for almost nine years, and when the Allies invaded Italy in 1944, Genovese helped the cause as a translator and facilitator while running the enormous black market. But on August 22, 1944, Military Police cracked down on the ring and arrested Genovese. An investigation into Genovese's background by Agent Orange C. Dickey of the Criminal Investigation Division of the US Army discovered that Genovese was a major criminal and wanted on murder charges in New York. Dickie made moves to have Genovese deported back to Manhattan to faces charges, but none of his superiors was interested in pressing the issue. After months of frustration, Dickey finally arranged to ship Genovese back to New York to face trial and that's when the pressure began. Dickey, who made less than $210 per month, turned down a bribe of $250,000 to let Genovese go. When that didn't work, pressure was brought down from high above to drop the case but Dickey refused.

Vito Genovese (right) with Salvatore Giuliano (left). Genovese

Genovese returned to New York in 1945, handcuffed to Agent Orange, and was immediately handed over to Brooklyn DA. But, by that time, the case was dropped because the state's witness, a hood named Pete LaTempa, was dead, killed while in protective custody at the Raymond Street jail in Manhattan.

Someone learned that LaTempa suffered from stomach ulcers, and on January 14, 1945, he was supplied with his usual dose of painkiller medicine before going

42

to sleep. The next morning he was found dead. A New York toxicologist analyzed his internal organs and reported that he had been given enough poison "to kill eight horses."

With the LaTempa problem behind him, by the fall of 1951, Vito Genovese was ready to begin his assault on Frank Costello and realize his dream of becoming the capo di tutti capi, the boss of all bosses. But a direct assault on Costello, an enormously powerful boss with deep political connections, would be suicidal. It was better to begin his campaign by eliminating one of Frank Costello's closest friends and allies and provoking Costello into a war for control of the family. He would start by having Willie Moretti murdered.

Morretti, an otherwise colorful hood, kept a low profile, mostly sticking to his expansive rackets in Northern New Jersey and Newark, where he ran a small, but effective gang out of Duke's Restaurant in Cliffside Park, New Jersey, a town that Morretti virtually owned because he was paying the local police chief and Mayor five times their annual income from the city.

Genovese's choice in picking Morretti as the ploy to start the gang war was perfect. Morretti and Frank Costello were close. Costello had been Moretti's best man at his wedding and was godfather to one of his children. Costello also shared in the two million dollar gambling business Morretti had built, making him rich and a loyal, and powerful, defender of the Costello regime. Costello had ensured that all of his Captains were rich but depended on his considerable political contacts to keep them rich and out of jail. As a result, aside from Morretti, Costello could count on the other Capos: Trigger Mike Copolla, Augie Carfano, Dominick DeQuatro, Jimmy Angelina, Tommy Greco, Richie Boiardi and Jimmy Blue Eyes Alo and the financial and management genius of Meyer Lansky.

For his part, Genovese could count on only three capos to support him a war: Jerry Catena, Mike Miranda, and Tony Bender. Bender and Genovese were also close. They married their wives in a joint ceremony in 1932, with Genovese acting as Bender's best man and vice versa. Yet, years later, while Genovese was in Atlanta Penitentiary, he told his cell mate, informant Joe Valachi, that Tony had "disappeared," that is, was murdered on Genovese's orders because Bender was sick with cancer and would never make his prison sentence and rather than risk his turning informant, Genovese Vito had him killed.

Mike Miranda (right) with Genovese

Mike Miranda

What Genovese needed to switch the Capos over to his side would be something to show that Costello wasn't acting in the best interest of the family, and Willie Morretti gave him the opening he needed to sow the seeds of doubt, and, as his luck should have it, the Kefauver Committee, a federal committee looking into the power of organized crime, arrived just in time to serve his needs.

Kefauver Committee in Chicago

On March 13, 1951, Frank Costello began his testimony before the committee in Manhattan. He had been forced to appear by subpoena and his attorney insisted that TV cameras present in the room did not focus directly on his client. Instead, he insisted, they were to be trained onto Costello's hands.

Kefauver

The committee meets, Frank Costello is seated at the left

The committee agreed and an estimated 30 million Americans watched in fascination, as Costello's hands danced across the screen, hour after hour.

There is no evidence that Vito Genovese provided information to the committee on Frank Costello, but the fact is, Kefauver had an enormous amount of inside information about the Prime Minister of the Underworld.

Costello was grilled on his name change, on his arrest background, on his naturalization proceedings, his bootlegging years.

Costello

Costello more or less answered everything, but when asked for a complete financial statement of his assets, he invoked the Fifth Amendment.

The committee's grilling of Costello went on until March 15, when Costello, complaining of a bad throat and laryngitis, walked out of the courtroom. When the hearings resumed on the March 19, the committee dug into Costello's considerable political connections and his close friendship with former New York Mayor O'Dwyer who was then the US Ambassador to Mexico. At one point in the hearings, Kefauver asked Costello, "How can we curb gambling in this country?" "Senator," Costello answered, "if you want to cut out gambling there's just two things you need to do. Burn the stables and shoot the horses."

When asked how he raised the money to finance the purchase of his three office buildings on Wall Street, he explained he had *"borrowed it from gamblers."*

The final day that he appeared, March 21, Senator Halley asked about Costello meeting with Lucky Luciano in Havana.

The Godfather didn't deny he was there, and explained he had been in Miami on business and had gone to Cuba for a brief vacation and "bumped into Charlie Lucky by accident." Halley tried desperately to connect Costello to Meyer Lansky and Jimmy Blue Eyes Alo but Costello avoided any direct connection to them.

Although an enormous number of mobsters appeared before the committee, it was Frank Costello who emerged as the best-known gangster in the nation and as a result he became a major target of the Justice Department, much to the pleasure of Vito Genovese.

Willie Moretti also appeared before the committee. As Genovese knew, Moretti was also a womanizer who had a liking for low-cost prostitutes, the darker and the younger, the better. Eventually, he developed syphilis, which went untreated and began to advance to the gangster mind and into his nervous system. He began to act strangely, doing and saying things that troubled the underworld, especially now that he had been called before the Kefauver committee.

Under oath, Moretti admitted that he was a gambler, that he knew Costello, Genovese and Adonis and every other big name gangster in the country and, further, that he was proud of those associations. He finished his testimony by inviting the committee to visit him at his home down on the Jersey shore. After that, he became something of a media celebrity, holding spur of the moment press conferences, giving reporters his opinion about the state of the world and even how to curb the growing power of the mob. Moretti was becoming an embarrassment to Costello and a minor danger to what would become the Genovese family. Vito Genovese saw the opening he was looking for. He quietly and cunningly began to spread rumors within the family and the ever-paranoid mob, that Willie Moretti was a security risk for everyone and said that Frank Costello was wrong to protect Moretti. But the real reason Genovese wanted Moretti dead, aside from ruining Costello's position within the family, was to take control of his lucrative gambling assets, a move he had readied for by positioning one of his best men, Jerry Catena, to take over as soon as Moretti was killed. With control of the gambling rackets, Genovese would have enough money to fight Costello for control of the family.

Willie Moretti outside the Kefauver hearings, joking with the press. The appearance cost him his life

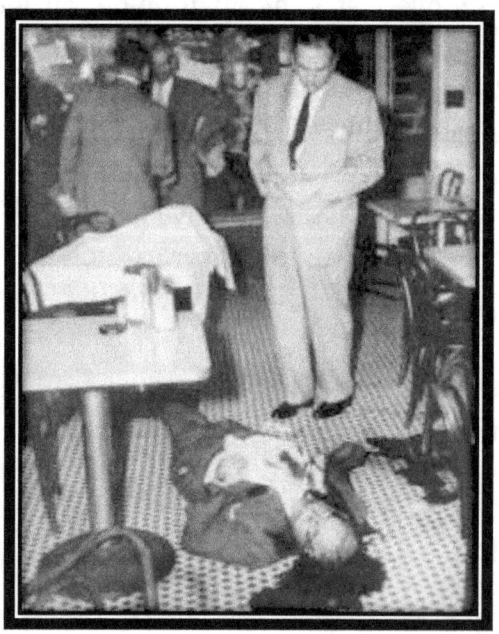

Moretti dead on the floor

Costello fought it, but the National Commission approved Willie Moretti's execution. At nine a.m. on October 4, 1951, Albert Anastasia, who lived in Fort

Lee, New Jersey, telephoned Moretti at his home and said that he had back troubles, and needed to go for x-rays but his chauffeur wasn't available. He asked if he could use Harry Shepherd, Moretti's driver and ever-faithful bodyguard. Moretti agreed.

Later that morning, Moretti, alone and unarmed, drove to Joe's Elbow Room Restaurant in suburban Cliffside, New Jersey, where three men were waiting for him. Moretti joined them at their table and the group spoke in Italian. Suddenly one of the men drew a revolver and shot Willie Moretti twice in the forehead, leaving his body sprawled on the patterned linoleum, between two tables.

After the success of the Moretti power play, Vito Genovese decided that the time had come to go after Frank Costello himself.

Following his appearance at the Kefauver hearings, the Federal Government charged Costello with a contempt of the Senate charge following his walk-out in the Kefauver hearings. Costello eventually went before two juries; the first ending in a hung jury, but the second resulting in an eighteen-month sentence that he began in August of 1952 and finished in October of 1953.

While Costello was in prison, in the summer of 1952, the IRS mounted a full-scale investigation against him. Agents checked every bank he and his wife went to, they interviewed his tailor, his barbershop, they staked out the restaurants he used. They traveled the country from Miami to New Orleans looking for leads but came up empty handed, unable to find a trace of any substantial undeclared income. Then, following one of his wife's checks, the agents found a shop that had supplied flowers to St. Michael's Cemetery in Astoria, Queens. There, on a plot purchased for $4,888, they found a marble mausoleum owned by Costello and built for his family for a total of $23,503, paid in cash through a friend named Amilicare Festa. The IRS was able to prove, eventually, that the money for the plot and the mausoleum came from Costello and in April of 1954, Costello went on trial for tax evasion. He was found guilty and sentenced to five years in prison and fined $30,000, the maximum penalty the law allowed. Costello fought the sentence all the way to the Supreme Court, which upheld his conviction and Costello was returned to prison on May 14, 1956. But, the following year, he hired the brilliant Edward Bennett Williams, and in April 1957, Williams secured Costello's release on parole. However, the Immigration department moved in and started denaturalization proceedings against him, which he fought for years.

All of this, Costello's jail time and endless legal problems, gave Genovese all the time he needed to plot and plan Costello's overthrow. On May 2, 1957, as

Costello returned to his apartment, a young thug named Vincent "The Chin" Gigante, who was working for Vito Genovese, walked up behind the Costello, and standing less than six feet away, pointed a pistol at him and said: "This is for you Frank," and then fired one shot at Costello's skull.

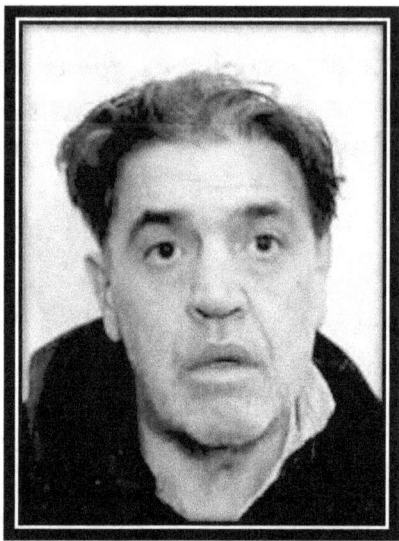

Vincent the Chin Gigante

But remarkably, he missed. The bullet tore into the skin behind Costello's right ear, ricocheted around the nape of his neck and slammed into the wall behind him. Gigante was long gone by the time Costello fell on the floor. He had run through the lobby and leaped into a waiting black Cadillac and disappeared into the night.

Costello after the near miss

Costello knew who ordered the attempted assassination and why. It was Vito Genovese, Costello's under boss. He had finally decided to make his move. To justify the shooting, a week before, Genovese called in his Capos, Tony Bender and Vincent Mauro and told them that Costello was an informer, and that was why he had been released early from prison.

Capo Tony Bender

The family got ready for war. However, nothing happened and then one by one Costello's lieutenants marched into Genoese's office and one by one said that they recognized him as the boss. Finally Costello sent out the message that he didn't want to fight. He was leaving the rackets. He had Made several fortunes and he wanted to spend the rest of his life in peace and quiet. Genovese agreed to let Costello leave the racket and to keep his life as well, but first he reduced Costello to the rank of a street soldier, stripped him of his gambling interests in Las Vegas, Florida and the Caribbean and made him turn over his points, or interests, in The Copacabana nightclub.

However, the war wasn't over. There was only one last thing in the way of Vito Genovese and that was Albert Anastasia. Back in the 1930's, when Lucky Luciano approached Anastasia about his plot to kill Joe the Boss Masseria and take over the mob, Anastasia, desperate for power, pushed Luciano to launch the plan. When it was successful, Luciano rewarded Anastasia for his loyalty by naming him under boss to the Mangano family under Vincent Mangano. However, in 1951, Anastasia grew tired of Mangano, and with Frank Costello's support, he had Mangano and his brother Phil shot to death and took over the family.

So while Frank Costello might have accepted his fate at Genoese's hands, Anastasia didn't. Anastasia went to the Commission members and openly accused Genovese of an illegal hit on Costello, and he began to talk about going to war with Genovese, a war to reinstate Costello to power, a war that he would probably win. Then Genovese learned that Costello and Anastasia were meeting secretly, and he panicked. He would have to kill Anastasia, before Anastasia killed him, but he would need the permission of the national commission, the shot taken at Costello had taught him that much.

Getting the commission's permission wasn't difficult. For them, Anastasia had grown too ambitious and was talking about ruling over all of New York and Las Vegas, which is exactly what all the other bosses wanted but feared to try to do. Anastasia had no such fears. In fact, he had already made a grab at the narcotics and gambling cash that was flowing out of Havana's from Lansky's racket and into the pockets of various Mafia and syndicate bosses across the globe.

Anastasia's mistake was inviting Cuba's other crime boss, Santos Trafficante, to join him in his efforts to take over the underworld. Trafficante could hand Cuba over to Anastasia, without his having to go through Lansky and Alo, who may have already entered an agreement with Genovese. Trafficante heard Anastasia out and told he needed to think about his offer. Instead, to protect his own assets in Cuba, Trafficante went straight to Genovese and cut his own deal. In turn, Genovese, with Trafficante behind him, took Anastasia's plan to the national commission who sanctioned the hit.

Genovese contacted Carlo Gambino, the cunning and ambitious capo under Anastasia, and convinced him that they would both benefit by murdering Anastasia. Gambino agreed and set up the hit.

Carlo Gambino

On October 25, 1957, the Gallo brothers killed Anastasia as he sat in the barbershop's chair at the Sheraton Hotel, a hot towel wrapped around his face. There were eleven people in the tiny shop, five barbers, a manicurist, three shoe shine boys and two customers who watched the two young hoods quickly enter the shop and put at least ten bullets into his head and neck.

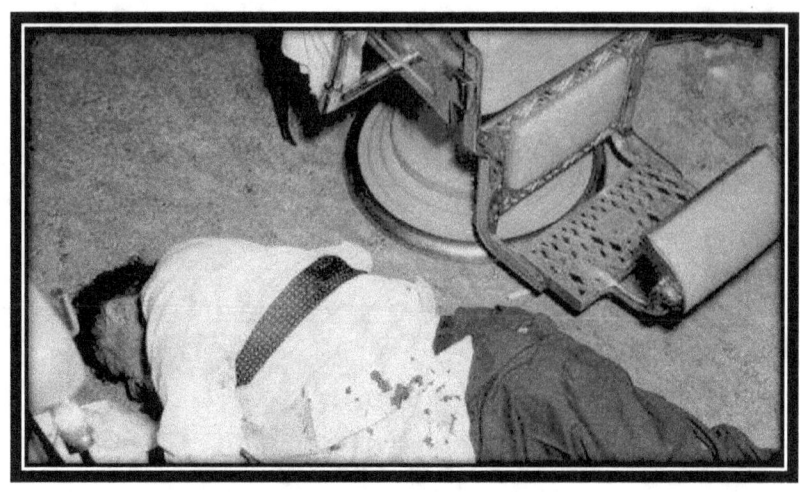

Anastasia, the Mad Hatter, dead

There was no big dollar, flashy mobster funeral for Anastasia. In fact, the mob barely showed up at all. Instead, his family attended the simple ceremony. Anastasia's wife Elsa, who married him in 1937 at age nineteen always refused to believe that her husband was a Mafia killer.   The Anastasia she knew never drank, was home by 9 p.m. and took the children to see movies "I never heard him say a bad word in front of me or the children. He never spoke roughly. He used to go to church with me every Sunday. He gave generously to the church... Now he's not even buried in consecrated ground."

After Vito Genovese took over the Luciano organization from Frank Costello, he was in almost complete control of half of New York's underworld, and all that Genovese needed was official recognition by the national commission as head of his family, and for Carlo Gambino as head of the Anastasia family. In time, both men would name their organizations after themselves, the Gambino and Genovese crime families.

Carlo Gambino liked to play the role of the gentle, non-violent, reasonable man but he was a crafty survivor and a cunning hood who positioned himself into becoming one of the most powerful and influential hoodlums who ever lived.

Born in Palermo on August 24, 1900, Carlo arrived in the United States (an illegal alien) in 1921. He resided in Brooklyn, assisted by numerous relatives who had arrived earlier. In turn, he helped his brothers Paolo (Paul), born 1904, and Giuseppe (Joseph), born 1908, when they arrived in the US. His boyhood friend from Palermo, Gaetano Lucchese, was already in the US and rising in the ranks of OC, first under Masseria and then, as a defector, under Maranzano.

Gambino, who was nominally on the side of "Joe the Boss," appears not to have actively participated in the Castellmarese War. He followed Lucchese into the Maranzano camp and after Maranzano's death moved into the ranks of the Mineo Family, eventually becoming a caporegime under Vincent Mangano.

Young Gambino, although he arrived in the states with the status of a Mafia prince, worked in the Castellano family during prohibition in a number of unglamorous positions as a rumrunner, a driver and shotgun guard. In the late 1920s, he was moved over to the powerful Masseria operations as bootlegger just in time for the Castellamarese War. After Luciano divided up New York into families, Gambino was assigned to Vincent Mangano and worked Brooklyn wharfs under Albert Anastasia.

Vincent Mangano

In 1931, Gambino was promoted to Capo and given his own crew to run. Now stable, at age 30, Gambino married his first cousin, Catherine Castellano. They raised four children, three sons and one daughter. The family lived in a modest, but expensively furnished row house in Brooklyn, all of it within Gambino's image low-key image.

When Prohibition ended, Gambino moved into contraband liquor, but was arrested for tax evasion. He walked from the charge because the evidence gathered against him had been taken from illegal phone wiretaps. Unlike most of the early hoods who died broke, Gambino was careful with his money and quietly invested in what were then taboo lines like a few dozen Gay bars for Homosexuals and lesbians, importing pornography and financing a narcotics network out of Montreal, Canada.

During the Second World War, Gambino, his brother Paul and New Jersey mobster Settimo "Big Sam" Accardi made millions from stealing and selling food and gas rationing stamps.

Accardi

Gambino was so successful at creating a black market for the stamps that he was eventually able to bring in corrupt members of the federal stamp-rationing program as partners in the deal. He invested that money into more than a hundred legitimate businesses which he owned outright or through fronts, including retail stores, super market markets, Restaurants and bar supply companies. He also owned the SGS Associates Public and Labor Relations firm, which solved labor disputes for some of New York's major real estate corporations. The firm closed after an investigation by state and federal authorities

In 1962, Gambino further solidified his power in the Underworld when his eldest son Tommy married the daughter of powerful mob boss Thomas Lucchese.

Lucchese

His other sons ran trucking businesses in New York's garment district. In 1970, when the Gambino Family ruled over 25 crews with more than 850 men, the Don was indicted for conspiracy to hijack an armored car carrying over $3 million dollars. Again, claiming poor health, he beat the legal system, however, several months later; the Supreme Court upheld a 1967 deportation order against him. Gambino finally killed off the deportation with a massive payment to a Democratic US Senator.

In 1971, Gambino's cherished wife died and the Don fell into a long but subtle depression. His health failed him and he more or less withdrew from the daily operations of the families far reaching business enterprises. He was the last of kind, for the American Mafia and the mighty Gambino family. The only serious tactical mistake that Gambino made in long career was to leave an oversized hood named Big Paul Castellano as his heir.

Big Paulie Castellano

Frank Costello, the boss deposed by Genovese, would have his revenge on Vito Genovese. But in doing so, he would be largely responsible for the start of the demise of the American Mafia. Like virtually everyone else in the mob, Meyer Lansky and Jimmy Blue Eyes Alo detested and feared Vito Genovese, a man they had both known for almost forty years, and once Frank Costello was gone, they had no intention of serving under him.

Jimmy Blue Eyes Alo

A few months after Genoese's public humiliation of Frank Costello, there was a secret meeting between Costello, Meyer Lansky and Jimmy Alo. A plan was mapped out to send Genovese away to federal prison on the toughest rap of all, narcotics.

The character Johnny Ola in the film, The Godfather Part 2, was said to be based on Jimmy Alo (Ola spelled backwards)

To set up the fall, they used a low-level Puerto Rican drug dealer named who was already doing five years at Sing on a drug charge. Cantellops was perfect for the role because the Feds had already tied him in to Sam Giancana in Chicago, and Giuseppe "Big Johnny" Ormerto, a Genovese family Capo. They also had information that Cantellops acted as a courier for Lansky.

Jimmy Alo

Jimmy "Blue Eyes" Alo sent a representative up to Sing Sing to offer Cantellops a deal, he would contact the Narcotics Bureau, Lansky supplied a name of an agent in the Bureau who was ready to take the complaint, and tell them that he had evidence to implicate Genovese in a major drug deal. If Cantellops went along, he would get $100,000 in cash, the money put up by Lansky, and Costello's lawyer would arrange to have his sentence annulled.

Cantellops took the offer, and in July of 1958, a grand jury was called in Manhattan, and Vito Genovese and 23 others were indicted for conspiracy to traffic in drugs. It was one of the weakest cases that the government ever presented before a court, but, on April 17, 1959, Genovese was convicted, fined $20,000 and sentenced to fifteen years in prison. The Godfather had his revenge.

Luciano and Costello were the last great leaders of the family that would come to bear the Genovese name. As for Don Vito Genovese, he got his power, but it was bittersweet. He died in prison in 1969.

www.ingramcontent.com/pod-product-compliance
Lightning Source LLC
Chambersburg PA
CBHW081855280526
45789CB00007B/2716